Church of England Marriage Services
with selected hymns, readings and prayers

Church of England Marriage Services

with selected hymns, readings and prayers

 CHURCH HOUSE PUBLISHING

Church House Publishing
Church House
Great Smith Street
London SW1P 3AZ

ISBN 978 0 7151 4202 8

Published 2010 by Church House Publishing

Typeset by
RefineCatch Limited, Bungay Suffolk

Printed in England by
CPI William Clowes, Beccles, NR34 7TL

Contents

Introduction

For the couple

Preparing for your wedding in the Church of England

If you are preparing to get married in the Church of England, then this book is for you. It contains the words of the two most commonly used Marriage Services, selections of readings from the Bible and elsewhere, and some wedding hymns and prayers. As part of the preparation for marriage, your priest will want to talk with you about the various options for your service and help you make decisions about what to include.

Because a Church of England wedding is a legal ceremony as well as a religious service (the priest acts as the registrar on behalf of the state), certain parts of the service are governed by law and cannot be changed. These include the necessary legal words: the declarations you will make – and also the vows: the promises you will make to one another before God. Couples sometimes ask whether they may write their own marriage vows. The answer is that only those words which have been authorized by the Church may be used. This is because these vows express a view of Christian marriage which is held and has been agreed by the whole Church.

There are, however, plenty of opportunities to make the wedding service personal. Readings from the Bible (and possibly from elsewhere) may be selected, and music (both hymns and instrumental pieces) may be chosen. Sometimes these elements of the service can offer an opportunity for friends or family members to be involved.

This book is designed to help you think about some of those possibilities and to discuss them with your priest as you prepare for your wedding.

Before the 'big day' there will be an opportunity to have a rehearsal in church. It is helpful if, for this rehearsal, as many as possible of those with a major role in the service can be present. This would normally include:

- the best man
- the chief bridesmaid/matron of honour
- the bride's father (if the bride is being 'given away')
- anyone doing a reading or leading prayers.

The rehearsal is a great opportunity to run through the entire service: all the words and the movement into, out of and within the church building. You will be able to ask questions about seating, about who moves and when, and you will be able to practise saying your vows and get used to the sound of your voices in the church. All this means that, on the day, you can relax and enjoy the service, without having to worry about the detail.

The Introduction to the Marriage Service in *Common Worship* reminds us that

A wedding is one of life's great moments, a time of solemn commitment as well as good wishes, feasting and joy.

We hope this book will help you plan effectively for your 'great moment' and that your wedding will mark the beginning of a joyful married life together.

For the minister

GENERAL INTRODUCTION FOR THE MINISTER

Marriages are one of the great joys of ministry – involvement in the life of a couple at a critical time is an enormous privilege. The Church of England's commitment to pastoral services is second to none: a clear statement of belief that the Christian gospel speaks into all parts of life and to all people, regardless of their religious commitment.

Church of England Marriage Services

Although fewer couples choose to marry in church than did in previous generations, significant numbers still opt for a church wedding. Some might do so because of a strong personal faith, some for reasons of 'tradition', but many choose to be married in church because they see it as the 'proper' thing to do and want to affirm the importance of a spiritual dimension to their life together.

A good marriage service begins months beforehand. Before meeting with the couple, it's important to be clear about the range of authorized services and the various options available. The Church of England has three authorized Marriage Services:

- the 1662 *Book of Common Prayer* service
- the service issued as one of the Alternative Services: Series One
- the *Common Worship* Marriage Service.

The first two use 'traditional language'; the third is cast in contemporary language.

The Church's Marriage Services are governed by law. They are authorized texts and it is important that they are used as such. When we sign registers, we confirm that we have married a couple 'according to the rites and ceremonies of the Church of England'. To depart from an authorized Marriage Service could therefore raise questions about the legality of a marriage. This being said, there are significant opportunities for the 'customization' of weddings. Research has shown that a priest taking time to make a marriage service 'personal' is one of the things most greatly valued by couples. During the pre-service meetings and preparation, we can talk about the choices of readings and music and help a couple make the service their own. There is room for flexibility – within the law!

Those places in the service which require the use of an authorized text are shown on pages 2–3. But the following are some 'soft points' within marriage liturgy:

- The Welcome (p. 5) – *Common Worship* offers suggested words for this, but there is freedom to use other appropriate words at the minister's discretion.

- The Readings (pp. 32–44).
- The Prayers (pp. 70–76).
- Hymns and songs (pp. 47–67).

We can also help personalize a service by offering to produce a customized Order of Service (perhaps with an image of the church on it). This is also a way in which, in a climate of escalating spending, a church can help keep a couple's costs down. We can talk with the couple about the design of the Order of Service – is there scope to include more than just section headings and the words of hymns? Some (or all) of the 'Pastoral Introduction' to the service from *Common Worship* might be included, perhaps with the text of one of the readings.

The wedding rehearsal before the day itself is a real gift – it helps the couple become more familiar with the building, gain confidence, and work through any practical questions before the big day. It also helps the minister get to know the other 'main players' by name.

The rehearsal can enable the bride and groom to do a full 'walk through' of the service, and give them the opportunity to rehearse parts of the service more than once if they wish, particularly any movement within the church building. Couples are often anxious about speaking during the service; the rehearsal lets them get used to the sound of their own voices in a large space. And above all, we can assure the couple – by giving clear instructions with a lightness of touch – that they don't need to worry but can relax and enjoy their wedding day.

When it comes to 'staging' a wedding, it is always worth asking questions about how the worship space is to be used:

- Where will the bride and groom stand to make their declarations and vows, and which way will they face to make them?
- Where will they sit for the readings and sermon?
- Where will the Registers be signed? (There is much to be said for signing them in the body of the church where everyone can see.)
- Will the couple move (perhaps to the high altar) for the prayers?

Church of England Marriage Services

A Marriage Service speaks very clearly of transformation as two become one through the joining of hands and the exchange of vows and rings. How might the drama of this transformation best be communicated? Possibilities might include:

- The lighting of a single large wedding candle by both bride and groom
- Vows being spoken (either learned or read) rather than repeated after the minister
- A 'staged rite' with movement from one part of the building to another at different sections of the service
- If either the bride or the groom is from another culture, it might be possible to incorporate a ceremonial custom from that culture within the service.

Remember to think about visibility for the congregation. The visual elements (e.g. joining together the couple's hands) need to be seen to have a proper impact.

This book includes the full text of the *Common Worship* (contemporary language) and the Series One (traditional language) Marriage Services, a selection of biblical and non-biblical readings, some hymns and prayers. It is designed to be both a handy-sized 'all-in-one' book for a minister, and also to be a book which can be given to couples who have booked their wedding, to help them make choices and prepare for the service.

Since 2007, the Church of England's *Weddings Project* has undertaken significant research into Church Weddings. As part of its work, it has set up the website www.yourchurchwedding.org which includes an online wedding planner. The hymn texts in this book are taken from those on the planner. They include some of the most popular hymns for church weddings and also some newer texts which may be sung to well-known tunes. The non-biblical readings include many which have become firm favourites, and the Bible readings are taken from the list of those suggested in *Common Worship: Pastoral Services*.

Marriage Services in the Church of England

For the couple

The Church of England has three authorized marriage services.

- The oldest of these is taken from the *Book of Common Prayer* and has been unchanged since 1662! It is written in what is often called 'traditional language' and reflects a view of marriage which some today might find old-fashioned.
- This service was revised in the twentieth century as *Alternative Services Series One: A Form of Solemnization of Matrimony* and it is this form that those couples who wish to have a traditional language service normally choose.
- The majority of Church of England weddings, though, use a service in modern English – *The Marriage Service: Common Worship* – which dates from 2000.

Your parish priest will be able to advise you on your choice of service as he or she helps you prepare for your marriage.

This book includes the full texts of both the *Series One* and *Common Worship* services.

For the minister

THE MARRIAGE SERVICE: COMMON WORSHIP

The *Common Worship* Marriage Service is the Church of England's contemporary language marriage service. It falls into two clear parts:

Church of England Marriage Services

¶ Introduction
   The Welcome
   Preface
   The Declarations
   The Collect
   Reading(s)
   Sermon

¶ The Marriage
   The Vows
   The Giving of Rings
   The Proclamation
   The Blessing of the Marriage
   Registration of the Marriage
   Prayers
   The Dismissal

Within this layout, the underlying shape of all *Common* Worship services may be seen: the service takes us on a journey which speaks of transformation: from an initial Gathering, through a hearing of God's word, to the marriage, prayer and dismissal. In this arrangement, the marriage *follows* the readings and sermon, emphasizing that the central action of any service takes place in response to God's word to us as revealed in Scripture. An option exists, though, for those who prefer, to solemnize the marriage earlier in the service, for the readings and sermon to follow the Blessing of the Marriage.

As we have seen, weddings include elements which – for legal reasons – are non-negotiable. Within the *Common Worship* service the following must be included, and in some cases the authorized wording has to be used (page numbers refer to this volume).

- The **Preface** (p. 6) – either this version or that on page 136 of *Common Worship: Pastoral Services* must be used
- The **Declarations** (p. 7) – the authorized wording must be used.
- The **Collect** (p. 8) must be included
- There must always be at least one **Reading from the Bible** (but see below)

- A **Sermon** is required, but the minister has freedom as to its style and content
- The **Vows** (p. 9) – the authorized wording must be used
- The **Giving of Rings** (p. 10) – the authorized wording must be used
- The **Proclamation** (p. 11) – the authorized wording must be used
- The **Blessing of the Marriage** (p. 11) – the wording on p. 11 or that on pp. 80–83 is used
- **The Lord's Prayer** (p. 14) must be included
- The **Dismissal** (p. 15).

The *Common Worship* Marriage Service*

¶ *Pastoral Introduction*

This may be read by those present before the service begins.

A wedding is one of life's great moments, a time of solemn commitment as well as good wishes, feasting and joy. St John tells how Jesus shared in such an occasion at Cana, and gave there a sign of new beginnings as he turned water into wine.

Marriage is intended by God to be a creative relationship, as his blessing enables husband and wife to love and support each another in good times and in bad, and to share in the care and upbringing of children. For Christians, marriage is also an invitation to share life together in the spirit of Jesus Christ. It is based upon a solemn, public and life-long covenant between a man and a woman, declared and celebrated in the presence of God and before witnesses.

On this their wedding day the bride and bridegroom face each other, make their promises and receive God's blessing. You are witnesses of the marriage, and express your support by your presence and your prayers. Your support does not end today: the couple will value continued encouragement in the days and years ahead of them.

Love is patient; love is kind; love is not envious or boastful or arrogant or rude. It does not insist on its own way; it is not irritable or resentful; it does not rejoice in wrongdoing, but rejoices in the truth. It bears all things, believes all things, hopes all things, endures all things.

I Corinthians 13.4-7

---

* A worked example of A Marriage Service with a Celebration of Holy Communion may be found on the Church of England web site at: www.cofe.anglican.org/worship/liturgy/commonworship/texts/marriage/marriagehc.html

---

Structure

¶ **Introduction**
The Welcome
Preface
The Declarations
The Collect
Readings
Sermon

¶ **The Marriage**
The Vows
The Giving of Rings
The Proclamation
The Blessing of the Marriage
Registration of the Marriage
Prayers
The Dismissal

¶ *Introduction*

The Welcome

The minister welcomes the people using these or other appropriate words

The grace of our Lord Jesus Christ,
the love of God,
and the fellowship of the Holy Spirit
be with you

All **and also with you.**

This sentence may be used

God is love, and those who live in love live in God
and God lives in them.

1 John 4.16

This prayer may be said

All   **God of wonder and of joy:**
grace comes from you,
and you alone are the source of life and love.
Without you, we cannot please you;
without your love, our deeds are worth nothing.
Send your Holy Spirit,
and pour into our hearts
   that most excellent gift of love,
that we may worship you now
with thankful hearts
and serve you always with willing minds;
through Jesus Christ our Lord.
Amen.

A hymn may be sung.

Preface

These words or those provided on page 136 of Common Worship:
Pastoral Services *are used*

In the presence of God, Father, Son and Holy Spirit,
we have come together
to witness the marriage of N and N,
to pray for God's blessing on them,
to share their joy
and to celebrate their love.

Marriage is a gift of God in creation
through which husband and wife may know the grace of God.
It is given
that as man and woman grow together in love and trust,
they shall be united with one another in heart, body and mind,
as Christ is united with his bride, the Church.

The gift of marriage brings husband and wife together
in the delight and tenderness of sexual union
and joyful commitment to the end of their lives.

It is given as the foundation of family life
in which children are [born and] nurtured
and in which each member of the family, in good times and in bad,
may find strength, companionship and comfort,
and grow to maturity in love.

Marriage is a way of life made holy by God,
and blessed by the presence of our Lord Jesus Christ
with those celebrating a wedding at Cana in Galilee.
Marriage is a sign of unity and loyalty
which all should uphold and honour.
It enriches society and strengthens community.
No one should enter into it lightly or selfishly
but reverently and responsibly in the sight of almighty God.

N and *N* are now to enter this way of life.
They will each give their consent to the other
and make solemn vows,
and in token of this they will [each] give and receive a ring.
We pray with them that the Holy Spirit will guide
    and strengthen them,
that they may fulfil God's purposes
for the whole of their earthly life together.

The Declarations

The minister says to the congregation

First, I am required to ask anyone present who knows a reason
why these persons may not lawfully marry, to declare it now.

The minister says to the couple

The vows you are about to take are to be made in the presence
    of God,
who is judge of all and knows all the secrets of our hearts;
therefore if either of you knows a reason why you may not
    lawfully marry,
you must declare it now.

The minister says to the bridegroom

N, will you take N to be your wife?
Will you love her, comfort her, honour and protect her,
and, forsaking all others,
be faithful to her as long as you both shall live?

He answers

I will.

The minister says to the bride

N, will you take N to be your husband?
Will you love him, comfort him, honour and protect him,
and, forsaking all others,
be faithful to him as long as you both shall live?

She answers

I will.

The minister says to the congregation

Will you, the families and friends of N and N,
support and uphold them in their marriage
now and in the years to come?

All   **We will.**

The Collect

*The minister invites the people to pray, silence is kept
and the minister says the Collect*

God our Father,
from the beginning
you have blessed creation with abundant life.
Pour out your blessings upon N and N,
that they may be joined in mutual love and companionship,
in holiness and commitment to each other.
We ask this through our Lord Jesus Christ your Son,
who is alive and reigns with you,
in the unity of the Holy Spirit,
one God, now and for ever.

All   **Amen.**

Readings

At least one reading from the Bible is used. A selection of readings is found on pages 32–39.

Sermon

¶ *The Marriage*

A hymn may be sung.
The couple stand before the minister.

The Vows

The minister introduces the vows in these or similar words

N and N, I now invite you to join hands and make your vows,
in the presence of God and his people.

The bride and bridegroom face each other.
The bridegroom takes the bride's right hand in his.
These words, or those on pages 78–79, are used

I, N, take you, N,
to be my wife,
to have and to hold
from this day forward;
for better, for worse,
for richer, for poorer,
in sickness and in health,
to love and to cherish,
till death us do part;
according to God's holy law.
In the presence of God I make this vow.

They loose hands.
The bride takes the bridegroom's right hand in hers, and says

I, N, take you, N,
to be my husband,
to have and to hold
from this day forward;
for better, for worse,

for richer, for poorer,
in sickness and in health,
to love and to cherish,
till death us do part;
according to God's holy law.
In the presence of God I make this vow.

They loose hands.

The Giving of Rings

The minister receives the ring(s), and says this prayer or the prayer on page 79

Heavenly Father, by your blessing
let *these rings be to N and N*
a symbol of unending love and faithfulness,
to remind them of the vow and covenant
which they have made this day
through Jesus Christ our Lord.

All   **Amen.**

The bridegroom places the ring on the fourth finger of the bride's left hand and, holding it there, says

N, I give you this ring
as a sign of our marriage.
With my body I honour you,
all that I am I give to you,
and all that I have I share with you,
within the love of God,
Father, Son and Holy Spirit.

If rings are exchanged, they loose hands and the bride places a ring on the fourth finger of the bridegroom's left hand and, holding it there, says

N, I give you this ring
as a sign of our marriage.
With my body I honour you,
all that I am I give to you,
and all that I have I share with you,
within the love of God,
Father, Son and Holy Spirit.

If only one ring is used, before they loose hands the bride says

N, I receive this ring
as a sign of our marriage.
With my body I honour you,
all that I am I give to you,
and all that I have I share with you,
within the love of God,
Father, Son and Holy Spirit.

The Proclamation

The minister addresses the people

In the presence of God, and before this congregation,
N and N have given their consent
and made their marriage vows to each other.
They have declared their marriage by the joining of hands
and by the giving and receiving of *rings*.
I therefore proclaim that they are husband and wife.

The minister joins their right hands together and says

Those whom God has joined together let no one put asunder.

The Blessing of the Marriage

*The husband and wife kneel. The minister may use the following blessing
or one of those on pages 80–83.*

Blessed are you, O Lord our God,
for you have created joy and gladness,
pleasure and delight, love, peace and fellowship.
Pour out the abundance of your blessing
upon N and N in their new life together.
Let their love for each other be a seal upon their hearts
and a crown upon their heads.
Bless them in their work and in their companionship;
awake and asleep,
in joy and in sorrow,
in life and in death.

Finally, in your mercy, bring them to that banquet
where your saints feast for ever in your heavenly home.
We ask this through Jesus Christ your Son, our Lord,
who lives and reigns with you and the Holy Spirit,
one God, now and for ever.

All **Amen.**

The minister says to the couple

God the Father,
God the Son,
God the Holy Spirit,
bless, preserve and keep you;
the Lord mercifully grant you the riches of his grace,
that you may please him both in body and soul,
and, living together in faith and love,
may receive the blessings of eternal life.

All **Amen.**

Registration of the Marriage

See Note 10 on page 16.

A hymn or psalm may be used.

Prayers

These or other suitable prayers are used (see Note 9 on page 16 and pages 70–76). The prayers usually include these concerns and may follow this sequence:

¶ *Thanksgiving*
¶ *Spiritual growth*
¶ *Faithfulness, joy, love, forgiveness and healing*
¶ *Children, other family members and friends*

Faithful God,
holy and eternal,
source of life and spring of love,
we thank and praise you for bringing N and N to this day,
and we pray for them.
Lord of life and love:

All   **hear our prayer.**

May their marriage be life-giving and life-long,
enriched by your presence and strengthened by your grace;
may they bring comfort and confidence to each other
in faithfulness and trust.
Lord of life and love:

All   **hear our prayer.**

May the hospitality of their home
bring refreshment and joy to all around them;
may their love overflow to neighbours in need
and embrace those in distress.
Lord of life and love:

All   **hear our prayer.**

May they discern in your word
order and purpose for their lives;
and may the power of your Holy Spirit
lead them in truth and defend them in adversity.
Lord of life and love:

All   **hear our prayer.**

May they nurture their family with devotion,
see their children grow in body, mind and spirit
and come at last to the end of their lives
with hearts content and in joyful anticipation of heaven.
Lord of life and love:

All   **hear our prayer.**

The prayers conclude with the Lord's Prayer.

As our Saviour taught us, so we pray

All **Our Father in heaven,**
hallowed be your name,
your kingdom come,
your will be done,
on earth as in heaven.
Give us today our daily bread.
Forgive us our sins
as we forgive those who sin against us.
Lead us not into temptation
but deliver us from evil.
For the kingdom, the power,
and the glory are yours
now and for ever.
Amen.

(or)

Let us pray with confidence as our Saviour has taught us

All **Our Father, who art in heaven,**
hallowed be thy name;
thy kingdom come;
thy will be done;
on earth as it is in heaven.
Give us this day our daily bread.
And forgive us our trespasses,
as we forgive those who trespass against us.
And lead us not into temptation;
but deliver us from evil.
For thine is the kingdom,
the power and the glory,
for ever and ever.
Amen.

A hymn may be sung.

The Dismissal

The minister says

God the Holy Trinity make *you* strong in faith and love,
defend *you* on every side, and guide *you* in truth and peace;
and the blessing of God almighty,
the Father, the Son, and the Holy Spirit,
be among *you* and remain with *you* always.

All   **Amen.**

Notes to the Marriage Service

1   Preparation

It is the custom and practice of the Church of England to offer preparation for marriage for couples who are soon to be married, as well as to be available for support and counselling in the years that follow.

2   The Banns

The banns are to be published in the church on three Sundays at the time of Divine Service by the officiant in the form set out in *The Book of Common Prayer* or in the following form:

I publish the banns of marriage between *NN* of . . . and *NN* of . . . This is the *first / second / third* time of asking. If any of you know any reason in law why they may not marry each other you are to declare it.

We pray for these couples (or *N* and *N*) as they prepare for their wedding(s).

A suitable prayer may be said (see page 135 in *Common Worship: Pastoral Services*).

3   Hymns and Canticles

These may be used at suitable points during the service.

4   Entry

The bride may enter the church escorted by her father or a representative of the family, or the bride and groom may enter church together.

5   Readings and Sermon

At least one reading from the Bible must be used. Suggested readings are printed on pages 32–39. If occasion demands, either the Sermon or the Readings and Sermon may come after the Blessing of the Marriage. Chairs may be provided for the bride and bridegroom.

6   'Giving Away'

This traditional ceremony is optional. Immediately before the couple exchange vows, the minister may ask:

Who brings this woman to be married to this man?

The bride's father (or mother, or another member of her family or a friend representing the family) gives the bride's right hand to the minister who puts it in the bridegroom's right hand. Alternatively, after the bride and bridegroom have made their Declarations, the minister may ask the parents of bride and bridegroom in these or similar words:

N and *N* have declared their intention towards each other.
As their parents,
will you now entrust your son and daughter to one another
as they come to be married?

Both sets of parents respond:

We will.

7   The Declarations and the Vows

The Book of Common Prayer version of the Declarations, and / or the alternative vows on pages 78–79, may be used. The couple repeat the vows after the minister, or may read them. If preferred, the question to the bride, and her vow, may come before the question to the bridegroom and his vow.

8   The Giving of Rings

If desired, the bride and bridegroom may each place a ring on the fourth finger of the other's hand, and may then say together the words 'N, I give you this ring . . .'. The prayer on page 79 may be used instead of the prayer on pages 10 and 11.

9   The Prayers

Several forms of intercession are provided. Other suitable forms may be used, especially prayers which the couple have written or selected in co-operation with the minister. Whatever form is used, silence may be kept as part of the intercession. Free prayer may be offered.

10 Registration of the Marriage

The law requires that the Registers are filled in immediately after the solemnization of a marriage. This may take place either after the Blessing of the Marriage or at the end of the service.

11 Holy Communion

For communicant members of the Church it is appropriate that they receive communion soon after their marriage. For some this may make it appropriate for the marriage to take place within the context of a Celebration of Holy Communion.

12 The Marriage Service within a Celebration of Holy Communion

The Notes to the Order for the Celebration of Holy Communion, as well as the Notes to the Marriage Service, apply equally to this service. Texts are suggested at different points, but other suitable texts may be used. Authorized Prayers of Penitence may be used. In the Liturgy of the Word, there should be a Gospel reading, preceded by either one or two other readings from the Bible. If desired, the Blessing of the Marriage may take place between the Lord's Prayer and the Breaking of the Bread.

13 Ecumenical Provisions

Where a minister of another Christian Church is invited to assist at the Solemnization of Matrimony, the permissions and procedures set out in Canon B 43 are to be followed. The Church of England minister who solemnizes the marriage must establish the absence of impediment, direct the exchange of vows, declare the existence of the marriage, say the final blessing, and sign the registers. A minister invited to assist may say all or part of the opening address, lead the declarations of intent, supervise the exchange of rings, and join in the blessing of the marriage. He or she may also read a lesson and lead all or part of the prayers. Where the couple come from different Christian communions the bishop may authorize such variations to the marriage service as are set out in An Order for the Marriage of Christians from Different Churches, which is published separately.

Alternative Services Series One:
A Form of Solemnization of Matrimony

For the minister

THE MARRIAGE SERVICE: SERIES ONE

The Church of England has two authorized Marriage Services in traditional language. One from the 1662 *Book of Common Prayer*, the other issued in 1966 as one of the Alternative Services: Series One. This Series One Service is an option for those who wish to use traditional language but without the *Book of Common Prayer*'s reference to 'brute beasts' and its insistence that marriage was ordained primarily 'as a remedy against sin'!

The service follows this pattern:

¶   Introduction: Preface and Declarations

¶   The Marriage: Vows and Giving of the Ring

¶   The Blessing of the Marriage: Psalm, Prayers and Blessing

A Collect, Epistle and Gospel are provided for when a Marriage is solemnized within a celebration of Holy Communion, and provision is made in the rubric for a Sermon (or some portion of Scripture) to follow the Blessing. In practice, many ministers will prefer to include the reading(s) and a sermon earlier in the service, possibly between the Marriage and the Prayers.

No reference is made to hymns, but these may be sung:

•   before the Introduction
•   between the Marriage and the Prayers
•   before the final Blessing.

Two forms of declaration for the bride are provided. The first includes the traditional *Book of Common Prayer* wording 'Wilt thou obey him, and serve him, love, honour and keep him. . . .'. The second amends this to 'Wilt thou love him, comfort him, honour and keep him. . . .' Likewise, two forms of the bride's vows are included. The first contains the traditional words 'and to obey' and the second omits them.

A Form of Solemnization of Matrimony*

At the day and time appointed for solemnization of matrimony, the persons to be married shall come into the body of the church with their friends and neighbours: and there standing together, the man on the right hand and the woman on the left, the priest shall say

¶ The Introduction

Dearly beloved, we are gathered here in the sight of God and in the face of this congregation, to join together this man and this woman in holy matrimony; which is an honourable estate, instituted of God himself, signifying unto us the mystical union that is betwixt Christ and his Church; which holy estate Christ adorned and beautified with his presence, and first miracle that he wrought, in Cana of Galilee, and is commended in Holy Writ to be honourable among all men; and therefore is not by any to be enterprised, nor taken in hand, unadvisedly, lightly, or wantonly; but reverently, discreetly, soberly, and in the fear of God, duly considering the causes for which matrimony was ordained.

First, it was ordained for the increase of mankind according to the will of God, and that children might be brought up in the fear and nurture of the Lord, and to the praise of his holy name.

Secondly, it was ordained in order that the natural instincts and affections, implanted by God, should be hallowed and directed aright; that those who are called of God to this holy estate, should continue therein in pureness of living.

Thirdly, it was ordained for the mutual society, help, and comfort, that the one ought to have of the other, both in prosperity and adversity.

Into which holy estate these two persons present come now to be joined.

---

* This service is virtually identical with the service in the Prayer Book proposed in 1928.

Therefore if any man can shew any just cause, why they may not lawfully be joined together, let him now speak, or else hereafter for ever hold his peace.

When two or more marriages are solemnized at the same time, all that follows, as far as the Psalm, shall be said in each case severally.

Speaking unto the persons that shall be married the priest shall say

I require and charge you both, as ye will answer at the dreadful day of judgement when the secrets of all hearts shall be disclosed, that if either of you know any impediment, why ye may not be lawfully joined together in matrimony, ye do now confess it. For be ye well assured, that so many as are coupled together otherwise than God's word doth allow are not joined together by God; neither is their matrimony lawful.

At which day of marriage, if any man do allege and declare any impediment, why they may not be coupled together in matrimony, by God's law, or the laws of this realm; then the solemnization must be deferred, until such time as the truth be tried.

¶ The Marriage

If no impediment be alleged, then shall the priest say unto the man

N, wilt thou have this woman to thy wedded wife, to live together according to God's law in the holy estate of matrimony? Wilt thou love her, comfort her, honour and keep her, in sickness and in health? and, forsaking all other, keep thee only unto her, so long as ye both shall live?

The man shall answer

I will.

Then shall the priest say unto the woman

(either)

N, wilt thou have this man to thy wedded husband, to live together after God's ordinance in the holy estate of matrimony? Wilt thou obey him, and serve him, love, honour, and keep him in sickness and in health; and, forsaking all other, keep thee only unto him, so long as ye both shall live?

(or)

N, wilt thou have this man to thy wedded husband, to live together according to God's law in the holy estate of matrimony? Wilt thou love him, comfort him, honour and keep him, in sickness and in health? and, forsaking all other, keep thee only unto him, so, long as ye both shall live?

The woman shall answer

I will.

Then shall the priest say

Who giveth this woman to be married to this man?

Then shall they give their troth to each other in this manner.

The priest, receiving the woman at her father's or friend's hands, shall cause the man with his right hand to take the woman by her right hand, and to say after him as follows

I, N, take thee, N, to my wedded wife, to have and to hold from this day forward, for better, for worse: for richer, for poorer; in sickness and in health; to love and to cherish, till death us do part, according to God's holy law; and thereto I give thee my troth.

Then shall they loose their hands; and the woman, with her right hand taking the man by his right hand, shall likewise say after the priest, one or other of these vows

I, N, take thee, N, to my wedded husband, to have and to hold from this day forward, for better for worse, for richer for poorer, in sickness and in health, to love, cherish, and to obey, till death us do part, according to God's holy ordinance; and thereto I give thee my troth.

(or)

I, N, take thee, N, to my wedded husband, to have and to hold from this day forward, for better, for worse: for richer, for poorer; in sickness and in health; to love and to cherish, till death us do part, according to God's holy law; and thereto I give thee my troth.

Then they shall again loose their hands; and the man shall give unto the woman a ring, laying the same upon the book.

Before delivering the ring the priest may say

Bless, O Lord, this ring, and grant that he who gives it and she who shall wear it may remain faithful to each other, and abide in thy peace and favour, and live together in love until their lives' end. Through Jesus Christ our Lord. Amen.

And the priest, taking the ring, shall deliver it to the man, to put it upon the fourth finger of the woman's left hand. And the man, holding the ring there, and taught by the priest, shall say

With this ring I thee wed; with my body I thee honour; and all my worldly goods with thee I share: In the name of the Father, and of the Son, and of the Holy Ghost. Amen.

Then shall the man leave the ring upon the fourth finger of the woman's left hand, and they shall both kneel down; but the people shall remain standing. Then shall the priest say

O Eternal God, Creator and Preserver of all mankind, giver of all spiritual grace, the author of everlasting life: send thy blessing upon these thy servants, this man and this woman, whom we bless in thy name; that, living faithfully together, they may surely perform and keep the vow and covenant betwixt them made, whereof this ring given and received is a token and pledge; and may ever remain in perfect love and peace together, and live according to thy laws; through Jesus Christ our Lord.

All   **Amen.**

Then shall the priest join their right hands together, and say

Those whom God hath joined together let no man put asunder.

Then shall the priest speak unto the people

Forasmuch as N and N have consented together in holy wedlock, and have witnessed the same before God and this company, and thereto have given and pledged their troth either to other, and have declared the same by giving and receiving of a ring, and by joining of hands; I pronounce that they be man and wife together, in the name of the Father, and of the Son, and of the Holy Ghost. Amen.

And the priest shall add this blessing

God the Father, God the Son, God the Holy Ghost, bless, preserve, and keep you; the Lord mercifully with his favour look upon you; and so fill you with all spiritual benediction and grace, that ye may so live together in this life, that in the world to come ye may have life everlasting.

All **Amen.**

¶ *The Blessing of the Marriage*

Then the priest, followed by the man and the woman, shall go to the Lord's table, while there is said or sung a psalm. The following are suitable:

Psalm 128 *Beati omnes*

1   Blessed are all they that fear the Lord :
   and walk in his ways.

2   For thou shalt eat the labour of thine hands :
   O well is thee, and happy shalt thou be.

3   Thy wife shall be as the fruitful vine :
   upon the walls of thine house;

4   Thy children like the olive-branches :
   round about thy table.

5   Lo, thus shall the man be blessed :
   that feareth the Lord.

6 The Lord from out of Sion shall so bless thee :
that thou shalt see Jerusalem in prosperity all thy life long;

7 Yea, that, thou shalt see thy children's children :
and peace upon Israel.

Glory be to the Father, and to the Son :
and to the Holy Ghost;
as it was in the beginning, is now, and ever shall be :
world without end. Amen.

Psalm 67 *Deus misereatur*

1 God be merciful unto us, and bless us :
and shew us the light of his countenance, and be
merciful unto us.

2 That thy way may be known upon earth :
thy saving health among all nations.

3 Let the people praise thee, O God :
yea, let all the people praise thee.

4 O let the nations rejoice and be glad :
for thou shalt judge the folk righteously,
and govern the nations upon earth.

5 Let the people praise thee, O God :
yea, let all the people praise thee.

6 Then shall the earth bring forth her increase :
and God, even our own God, shall give us his blessing.

7 God shall bless us :
and all the ends of the world shall fear him.

Glory be to the Father, and to the Son :
and to the Holy Ghost;
as it was in the beginning, is now, and ever shall be :
world without end. Amen.

Psalm 37.3-7 *Spera in Domino*

3   Put thou thy trust in the Lord, and be doing good :
    dwell in the land, and verily thou shalt be fed.

4   Delight thou in the Lord :
    and he shall give thee thy heart's desire.

5   Commit thy way unto the Lord, and put thy trust in him :
    and he shall bring it to pass.

6   He shall make thy righteousness as clear as the light :
    and thy just dealing as the noon-day.

7   Hold thee still in the Lord :
    and abide patiently upon him.

Glory be to the Father, and to the Son :
and to the Holy Ghost;
as it was in the beginning, is now, and ever shall be :
world without end. Amen.

*The psalm ended, the people kneeling, and the man and the woman
kneeling before the Lord's table, the priest standing at the table, and
turning his face towards them, shall say*

Let us pray.

Lord, have mercy upon us.

All   **Christ, have mercy upon us.**

Lord, have mercy upon us.

All   **Our Father, which art in heaven,**
hallowed be thy name;
thy kingdom come;
thy will be done,
in earth as it is in heaven.
Give us this day our daily bread.
And forgive us our trespasses,
as we forgive them that trespass against us.
And lead us not into temptation;
but deliver us from evil. Amen.

O Lord, save thy servant, and thy handmaid;

All **Who put their trust in thee.**

O Lord, send them help from thy holy place;

All **And evermore defend them.**

Be unto them a tower of strength;

All **From the face of their enemy.**

O Lord, hear our prayer,

All **And let our cry come unto thee.**

O God of our fathers, bless these thy servants, and sow the seed of eternal life in their hearts; that whatsoever in thy holy Word they shall profitably learn, they may in deed fulfil the same; that so, obeying thy will, and alway being in safety under thy protection, they may abide in thy love unto their lives' end; through Jesus Christ our Lord.

All **Amen.**

This prayer next following shall be omitted, where the woman is past child-bearing

O merciful Lord and heavenly Father, by whose gracious gift mankind is increased; bestow, we beseech thee, upon these two persons the heritage and gift of children; and grant that they may see their children christianly and virtuously brought up to thy praise and honour, through Jesus Christ our Lord.

All **Amen.**

This prayer shall follow

O God, who hast taught us that it should never be lawful to put asunder those whom thou by matrimony hadst made one, and hast consecrated the state of matrimony to such an excellent mystery, that in it is signified and represented the spiritual marriage and unity betwixt Christ and his Church: Look mercifully upon these thy servants, that both this man may love his wife, according to thy word (as Christ did love his spouse the Church, who gave himself for it, loving and cherishing it even as his own flesh,) and also that this woman may be loving and amiable, and faithful to her husband,

and in all quietness, sobriety, and peace, be a follower of holy and godly matrons. O Lord, bless them both, and grant them to inherit thy everlasting kingdom; through Jesus Christ our Lord.

All **Amen.**

Then shall the priest say this blessing

Almighty God, the Father of our Lord Jesus Christ, Pour upon you the riches of his grace, sanctify and bless you, that ye may please him both in body and soul, and live together in holy love unto your lives' end.

All **Amen.**

If there be a Communion, the foregoing prayer and blessing shall be said over the man and woman immediately before the final blessing of the congregation at the Communion.

If there be no Communion, here shall follow the sermon; or there shall be read some portion of Scripture. And then the priest shall dismiss those that are gathered, saying

Let us pray.

O almighty Lord, and everlasting God, vouchsafe, we beseech thee, to direct, sanctify, and govern, both our hearts and bodies, in the ways of thy laws, and in the works of thy commandments; that through thy most mighty protection, both here and ever, we may be preserved in body and soul; through our Lord and Saviour Jesus Christ.

All **Amen.**

The blessing of God Almighty, the Father, the Son, and the Holy Ghost, be amongst you and remain with you always.

All **Amen.**

¶ The Communion

If there be a Communion, the following Collect, Epistle, and Gospel, or the Collect, Epistle, and Gospel of the day, may be used immediately after the prayer for child-bearing; or after the Collect preceding it, if that be not said.

The Collect

O God our Father, who by thy holy Apostle hast taught us that love is the fulfilling of the law: Grant to these thy servants that, loving one another, they may continue in thy love unto their lives' end; through Jesus Christ our Lord, who liveth and reigneth with thee in the unity of the Holy Ghost, one God world without end.

All **Amen.**

The Epistle

For this cause I bow my knees unto the Father of our Lord Jesus Christ, of whom the whole family in heaven and earth is named, that he would grant you, according to the riches of his glory, to be strengthened with might by his Spirit in the inner man; that Christ may dwell in your hearts by faith; that ye, being rooted and grounded in love, may be able to comprehend with all saints what is the breadth, and length, and depth, and height; and to know the love of Christ, which passeth knowledge, that ye might be filled with all the fullness of God.

Ephesians 3.14-19

The Gospel

As the Father hath loved me, so have I loved you: continue ye in my love. If ye keep my commandments, ye shall abide in my love; even as I have kept my Father's commandments, and abide in his love. These things have I spoken unto you, that my joy might remain in you, and that your joy might be full. This is my commandment, That ye love one another, as I have loved you.

St. John 15.9-12

Readings

For the couple

Selecting Readings for your Wedding

One of the joys of planning a wedding service is making the choices (of music and readings) that help make the service personal.

All Church of England weddings must include at least one reading from the Bible. You will find a selection of Bible readings on pages 32–39. As well as a reading (or readings) from the Bible, it might be possible to include a reading from elsewhere. A selection of non-biblical readings is given on pages 40–44. When thinking about the choice of readings, it's important to discuss this at an early stage with the priest.

A reading is an excellent opportunity to involve a friend or family member in your wedding service. Three things are important, though:

- Check that the person is happy about reading in public.
- Make sure that, if possible, they can rehearse their reading in the building beforehand (and get used to any microphones there might be).
- Check that the priest is willing for them to read.

For the minister

READINGS FROM THE BIBLE

Common Worship is clear that, at a wedding, there must always be at least one reading from the Bible. A choice of suitable passages is printed in *Common Worship: Pastoral Services* (pp. 137–149) and a selection from these is printed here (pp. 32–39). However, we are not limited to these passages, and any appropriate Bible readings may be selected. If a marriage is to take place within a celebration of Holy Communion, there should be at least two readings from the Bible, the final one of which must be a Gospel reading.

The choice of readings is an area where there can be fruitful conversation between the minister and couple during preparation. The requirement (in the *Common Worship* service) that a sermon should be preached gives a further opportunity for developing themes from the reading.

It is often the case that at weddings, readings are read by family members or by friends of the couple. If this is so, then care needs to be taken that the reader is well-briefed about when and where to move during the service, and (if at all possible) is given the opportunity to practise in the building and become familiar with the sound system (if there is one).

OTHER READINGS

On the matter of non-biblical readings at weddings, *Common Worship* is silent. This silence means that, in addition to a reading or readings from the Bible, a non-biblical reading may be included in the service at the discretion of the minister.

The minister's discretion is essential: a non-biblical reading should support – and not contradict or undermine – the Christian view of marriage as the Church of England understands it. Before agreeing to the inclusion of a non-biblical reading the minister needs to be convinced about its suitability, and should ensure that the reading and its meaning are discussed with the couple during the preparation for the service.

Because *Common Worship* makes no mention of non-biblical readings, no guidance is given about where in the service they should come. There are various possibilities:

- The most obvious – and usual – place is as one of the Readings (p. 8). If this is the case, then it's important that the Bible 'should have the last word' – in other words, a non-biblical reading should precede a reading from the Bible. The sermon then provides an opportunity for the minister to draw together threads from both.

- A short non-biblical passage might be read between the opening Welcome and the Preface.
- A short reading might follow the Blessing of the Couple, before the Registration of the Marriage.

Bible readings

Any suitable translation may be used.

Old Testament and Apocrypha

Genesis 1.26-28

> Then God said, 'Let us make humankind in our image, according to
> our likeness; and let them have dominion over the fish of the sea,
> and over the birds of the air, and over the cattle, and over all the wild
> animals of the earth, and over every creeping thing that creeps upon
> the earth.'
>
> So God created humankind in his image,
> in the image of God he created them;
> male and female he created them.
>
> God blessed them, and God said to them, 'Be fruitful and multiply,
> and fill the earth and subdue it; and have dominion over the fish of
> the sea and over the birds of the air and over every living thing that
> moves upon the earth.'

Song of Solomon 2.10-13; 8.6,7

> My beloved speaks and says to me:
> 'Arise, my love, my fair one,
> and come away;
> for now the winter is past,
> the rain is over and gone.
> The flowers appear on the earth;
> the time of singing has come,
> and the voice of the turtle dove
> is heard in our land.
> The fig tree puts forth its figs,
> and the vines are in blossom;
> they give forth fragrance.

Arise, my love, my fair one,
and come away.'
Set me as a seal upon your heart,
as a seal upon your arm;
for love is strong as death,
passion fierce as the grave.
Its flashes are flashes of fire,
a raging flame.
Many waters cannot quench love,
neither can floods drown it.
If one offered for love
all the wealth of one's house,
it would be utterly scorned.

New Testament

Romans 12.1,2,9-13

I appeal to you therefore, brothers and sisters, by the mercies of God, to present your bodies as a living sacrifice, holy and acceptable to God, which is your spiritual worship. Do not be conformed to this world, but be transformed by the renewing of your minds, so that you may discern what is the will of God – what is good and acceptable and perfect.

Let love be genuine; hate what is evil, hold fast to what is good; love one another with mutual affection; outdo one another in showing honour. Do not lag in zeal, be ardent in spirit, serve the Lord. Rejoice in hope, be patient in suffering, persevere in prayer. Contribute to the needs of the saints; extend hospitality to strangers.

Romans 15.1-3,5-7,13

We who are strong ought to put up with the failings of the weak, and not to please ourselves. Each of us must please our neighbour for the good purpose of building up the neighbour. For Christ did not please himself; but, as it is written, 'The insults of those who insult you have fallen on me.'

May the God of steadfastness and encouragement grant you to live in harmony with one another, in accordance with Christ Jesus, so that together you may with one voice glorify the God and Father of our Lord Jesus Christ. Welcome one another, therefore, just as Christ has welcomed you, for the glory of God.

May the God of hope fill you with all joy and peace in believing, so that you may abound in hope by the power of the Holy Spirit.

I Corinthians 13

If I speak in the tongues of mortals and of angels, but do not have love, I am a noisy gong or a clanging cymbal. And if I have prophetic powers, and understand all mysteries and all knowledge, and if I have all faith, so as to remove mountains, but do not have love, I am nothing. If I give away all my possessions, and if I hand over my body so that I may boast, but do not have love, I gain nothing.

Love is patient; love is kind; love is not envious or boastful or arrogant or rude. It does not insist on its own way; it is not irritable or resentful; it does not rejoice in wrongdoing, but rejoices in the truth. It bears all things, believes all things, hopes all things, endures all things.

Love never ends. But as for prophecies, they will come to an end; as for tongues, they will cease; as for knowledge, it will come to an end. For we know only in part, and we prophesy only in part; but when the complete comes, the partial will come to an end. When I was a child, I spoke like a child, I thought like a child, I reasoned like a child; when I became an adult, I put an end to childish ways. For now we see in a mirror, dimly, but then we will see face to face. Now I know only in part; then I will know fully, even as I have been fully known. And now faith, hope, and love abide, these three; and the greatest of these is love.

Ephesians 3.14-end

I bow my knees before the Father, from whom every family in heaven and on earth takes its name. I pray that, according to the riches of his glory, he may grant that you may be strengthened in your inner being with power through his Spirit, and that Christ may dwell in your hearts through faith, as you are being rooted and grounded in love. I pray that you may have the power to comprehend, with all the saints, what is the breadth and length and height and depth, and to know the love of Christ that surpasses knowledge, so that you may be filled with all the fullness of God.

Now to him who by the power at work within us is able to accomplish abundantly far more than all we can ask or imagine, to him be glory in the church and in Christ Jesus to all generations, for ever and ever. Amen.

Ephesians 5.21-end

Be subject to one another out of reverence for Christ.

Wives, be subject to your husbands as you are to the Lord. For the husband is the head of the wife just as Christ is the head of the church, the body of which he is the Saviour. Just as the church is subject to Christ, so also wives ought to be, in everything, to their husbands.

Husbands, love your wives, just as Christ loved the church and gave himself up for her, in order to make her holy by cleansing her with the washing of water by the word, so as to present the church to himself in splendour, without a spot or wrinkle or anything of the kind – yes, so that she may be holy and without blemish. In the same way, husbands should love their wives as they do their own bodies. He who loves his wife loves himself. For no one ever hates his own body, but he nourishes and tenderly cares for it, just as Christ does for the church, because we are members of his body. 'For this reason a man will leave his father and mother and be joined to his wife, and the two will become one flesh.' This is a great mystery, and I am applying it to Christ and the church. Each of you, however, should love his wife as himself, and a wife should respect her husband.

Philippians 4.4-9

Rejoice in the Lord always; again I will say, Rejoice. Let your gentleness be known to everyone. The Lord is near. Do not worry about anything, but in everything by prayer and supplication with thanksgiving let your requests be made known to God. And the peace of God, which surpasses all understanding, will guard your hearts and your minds in Christ Jesus.

Finally, beloved, whatever is true, whatever is honourable, whatever is just, whatever is pure, whatever is pleasing, whatever is commendable, if there is any excellence and if there is anything worthy of praise, think about these things. Keep on doing the things that you have learned and received and heard and seen in me, and the God of peace will be with you.

Colossians 3.12-17

As God's chosen ones, holy and beloved, clothe yourselves with compassion, kindness, humility, meekness, and patience. Bear with one another and, if anyone has a complaint against another, forgive each other; just as the Lord has forgiven you, so you also must forgive. Above all, clothe yourselves with love, which binds everything together in perfect harmony. And let the peace of Christ rule in your hearts, to which indeed you were called in the one body. And be thankful. Let the word of Christ dwell in you richly; teach and admonish one another in all wisdom; and with gratitude in your hearts sing psalms, hymns, and spiritual songs to God. And whatever you do, in word or deed, do everything in the name of the Lord Jesus, giving thanks to God the Father through him.

1 John 4.7-12

Beloved, let us love one another, because love is from God; everyone who loves is born of God and knows God. Whoever does not love does not know God, for God is love. God's love was revealed among us in this way: God sent his only Son into the world so that we might live through him. In this is love, not that we loved

God but that he loved us and sent his Son to be the atoning sacrifice for our sins. Beloved, since God loved us so much, we also ought to love one another. No one has ever seen God; if we love one another, God lives in us, and his love is perfected in us.

Gospel

Mark 10.6-9, 13-16

Jesus said, 'From the beginning of creation, "God made them male and female." "For this reason a man shall leave his father and mother and be joined to his wife, and the two shall become one flesh." So they are no longer two, but one flesh. Therefore what God has joined together, let no one separate.'

People were bringing little children to him in order that he might touch them; and the disciples spoke sternly to them. But when Jesus saw this, he was indignant and said to them, 'Let the little children come to me; do not stop them; for it is to such as these that the kingdom of God belongs. Truly I tell you, whoever does not receive the kingdom of God as a little child will never enter it.' And he took them up in his arms, laid his hands on them, and blessed them.

John 2.1-11

On the third day there was a wedding in Cana of Galilee, and the mother of Jesus was there. Jesus and his disciples had also been invited to the wedding. When the wine gave out, the mother of Jesus said to him, 'They have no wine.' And Jesus said to her, 'Woman, what concern is that to you and to me? My hour has not yet come.' His mother said to the servants, 'Do whatever he tells you.' Now standing there were six stone water-jars for the Jewish rites of purification, each holding twenty or thirty gallons. Jesus said to them, 'Fill the jars with water.' And they filled them up to the brim. He said to them, 'Now draw some out, and take it to the chief steward.' So they took it. When the steward tasted the water that had become wine, and did not know where it came from (though the servants who had drawn the water knew), the steward called the bridegroom and said to him, 'Everyone serves the good wine first, and then the inferior wine after the guests have become drunk. But you have kept the good wine until now.' Jesus did this, the first of his signs, in Cana of Galilee, and revealed his glory; and his disciples believed in him.

John 15.9-17

Jesus said to his disciples: 'As the Father has loved me, so I have loved you; abide in my love. If you keep my commandments, you will abide in my love, just as I have kept my Father's commandments and abide in his love. I have said these things to you so that my joy may be in you, and that your joy may be complete.

This is my commandment, that you love one another as I have loved you. No one has greater love than this, to lay down one's life for one's friends. You are my friends if you do what I command you. I do not call you servants any longer, because the servant does not know what the master is doing; but I have called you friends, because I have made known to you everything that I have heard from my Father. You did not choose me but I chose you. And I appointed you to go and bear fruit, fruit that will last, so that the Father will give you whatever you ask him in my name. I am giving you these commands so that you may love one another.'

Psalms

Psalm 121

I lift up my eyes to the hills; •
from where is my help to come?

My help comes from the Lord, •
the maker of heaven and earth.

He will not suffer your foot to stumble; •
he who watches over you will not sleep.

Behold, he who keeps watch over Israel •
shall neither slumber nor sleep.

The Lord himself watches over you; •
the Lord is your shade at your right hand,

So that the sun shall not strike you by day, •
neither the moon by night.

The Lord shall keep you from all evil; •
it is he who shall keep your soul.

The Lord shall keep watch over your going out
    and your coming in, •
from this time forth for evermore.

Psalm 127

Unless the Lord builds the house, •
those who build it labour in vain.

Unless the Lord keeps the city, •
the guard keeps watch in vain.

It is in vain that you hasten to rise up early
    and go so late to rest, eating the bread of toil, •
for he gives his beloved sleep.

Children are a heritage from the Lord •
and the fruit of the womb is his gift.

Like arrows in the hand of a warrior, •
so are the children of one's youth.

Happy are those who have their quiver full of them: •
they shall not be put to shame
    when they dispute with their enemies in the gate.

Non-biblical readings

We are all on our own paths, all on our own journeys.
Sometimes the paths cross, and people arrive at the crossing
points at the same time and meet each other.
There are greetings, pleasantries are exchanged,
and then they move on.
But then once in a while the pleasantries become more, friendship
grows, deeper links are made, hands are joined and love flies.
The friendship has turned into love.
Paths are joined, one path with two people walking it, both
going in the same direction, and sharing each other's journeys.
Today N and N are joining their paths.
They will now skip together in harmony and love, sharing joys
and sorrows, hopes and fears, strengthening and upholding
each other as they walk along side by side.
At home by the fire, whenever I look up, there you will be.
And whenever you look up, there I shall be.

Adapted from *Far from the Madding Crowd*
Thomas Hardy

Your marriage should have within it a secret and protected space,
open to you alone. Imagine it to be a walled garden, entered by a
door to which you only hold the key. Within this garden you will
cease to be a mother, father, employee, homemaker or any other
of the roles which you fulfil in daily life. Here you can be
yourselves, two people who love each other. Here you can
concentrate on one another's needs. So take each other's hands
and go forth to your garden. The time you spend together is not
wasted but invested – invested in your future and nurture of your love.

A walled garden (author unknown)

What greater thing is there for two human souls than to feel that
they are joined – to strengthen each other – to be at one with each
other in silent unspeakable memories.

To be at one with each other
George Eliot

Never marry but for love; but see that thou lovest what is lovely.
He that minds a body and not a soul
has not the better part of that relationship,
and will consequently lack the noblest comfort of a married life.

Between a man and his wife nothing ought to rule but love.
As love ought to bring them together,
so it is the best way to keep them well together.

A husband and wife that love one another
show their children that they should do so too.
Others visibly lose their authority in their families
by their contempt of one another,
and teach their children to be unnatural by their own examples.

Let not enjoyment lessen, but augment, affection;
it being the basest of passions to like when we have not,
what we slight when we possess.

Here it is we ought to search out our pleasure,
where the field is large and full of variety, and of an enduring nature;
sickness, poverty or disgrace being not able to shake it
because it is not under the moving influences of worldly
    contingencies.

Nothing can be more entire and without reserve;
nothing more zealous, affectionate and sincere;
nothing more contented than such a couple,
nor greater temporal felicity than to be one of them.

William Penn

Let your love be stronger than your hate or anger.
Learn the wisdom of compromise,
for it is better to bend a little than to break.
Believe the best rather than the worst.
People have a way of living up or down to your opinion of them.
Remember that true friendship is the basis for any lasting relationship.
The person you choose to marry is deserving of the courtesies
and kindnesses you bestow on your friends.

Church of England Marriage Services

Please hand this down to your children and your children's children.

Marriage Advice
Jane Wells

How do I love thee? Let me count the ways.
I love thee to the depth and breadth and height
My soul can reach, when feeling out of sight
For the ends of Being and ideal Grace.
I love thee to the level of every day's
Most quiet need; by sun and candle-light.
I love thee freely, as men strive for Right;
I love thee purely, as they turn from Praise.
I love thee with the passion put to use
In my old griefs, and with my childhood's faith
I love thee with a love I seemed to lose
With my lost saints, I love thee with the breath.
Smiles, tears, of all my life! And, if God choose,
I shall but love thee better after death.

Sonnet from the Portuguese XLIII
Elizabeth Barrett Browning

All kings, and all their favourites,
All glory of honours, beauties, wits,
The sun itself, which makes times, as they pass,
Is elder by a year now than it was
When thou and I first one another saw:
All other things to their destruction draw,
Only our love hath no decay;
This no tomorrow hath, nor yesterday,
Running it never runs from us away,
But truly keeps his first, last, everlasting day.

From *The Anniversary*
John Donne

Let me not to the marriage of true minds
Admit impediments. Love is not love
Which alters when it alteration finds,
Or bends with the remover to remove:
O, no! it is an ever-fixed mark,
That looks on tempests and is never shaken;
It is the star to every wandering bark,
Whose worth's unknown, although his height be taken.
Love's not Time's fool, though rosy lips and cheeks
Within his bending sickle's compass come;
Love alters not with his brief hours and weeks,
But bears it out even to the edge of doom.
If this be error and upon me proved,
I never writ, nor no man ever loved.

> Sonnet 116: *Let Me Not to the Marriage of True Minds*
> William Shakespeare

Happiness in marriage is not something that just happens. A good marriage must be created. In marriage the little things are the big things. It is never being too old to hold hands. It is remembering to say 'I love you' at least once a day. It is never going to sleep angry. It is at no time taking the other for granted; the courtship should not end with the honeymoon, it should continue through all the years. It is having a mutual sense of values and common objectives. It is standing together facing the world. It is forming a circle of love that gathers in the whole family. It is doing things for each other, not in the attitude of duty or sacrifice, but in the spirit of joy. It is speaking words of appreciation and demonstrating gratitude in thoughtful ways. It is not looking for perfection in each other. It is cultivating flexibility, patience, understanding and a sense of humour. It is having the capacity to forgive and forget. It is giving each other an atmosphere in which each can grow. It is a common search for the good and the beautiful. It is establishing a relationship in which the independence is equal, dependence is mutual and the obligation is reciprocal. It is not only marrying the right partner, it is being the right partner.

> from *The Art of Marriage*
> Wilferd Arlan Peterson

Treat yourselves and each other with respect,
and remind yourselves often of what brought you together.
Give the highest priority to the tenderness, gentleness and kindness
that your connection deserves.
When frustration, difficulty and fear assail your relationship;
as they threaten all relationships at one time or another,
remember to focus on what is right between you,
not only the part which seems wrong.
In this way, you can ride out the storms
when clouds hide the face of the sun in your lives,
remembering that even if you lose sight of it for a moment,
the sun is still there.
And if each of you takes responsibility
for the quality of your life together,
it will be marked by abundance and delight.
Go now to your dwelling place,
to enter into the days of your life together.
And may your days be good and long upon the earth.

An Apache Wedding Prayer (author unknown)

Hymns

For the couple

Choosing hymns for your wedding

Most weddings in the Church of England include hymns for the congregation to sing. Hymns are one of the important ingredients which help turn a wedding into *your* wedding. Many couples choose hymns that have been special for them at key points in their life. It might be that you know and love a hymn that was sung at your confirmation, or at school, or which speaks to you about a particular aspect of the Christian faith.

But it's also important to choose hymns (or at least tunes) which the congregation will know and will be able to sing. In some churches, you might be fortunate enough to have the services of a choir; a good choir can help give confidence to a congregation's singing. If there is no choir, you need to be careful about choosing well-known hymns. (There's nothing worse than a wedding hymn which turns out to be a duet between the vicar and the organist!)

Sometimes 'less is more' where wedding hymns are concerned. It's far better to sing just two hymns well, than to have a congregation struggle its way through four. Talk about your choices when you meet with the priest to plan the service, and about where in the service the hymns might come.

The pages that follow contain a selection of suitable hymns. Some are time-honoured favourites and others offer newer words, all of which may be sung to well-known tunes. Some of these can be listened to as mp3 files at http://www.yourchurchwedding.org/hymns-media-player.aspx

For the minister

HYMNS

The choice of hymns and songs is an area where a couple has a real opportunity to make a service personal. Yet while some couples will have clear ideas about what they would like to sing, others will seem at a loss. The majority of those now being married in church have not grown up in a context in which hymn-singing has been part of their background. For many, the most significant hymns will be those they sang at their primary school.

It's important to remember that, whatever the preferences of the minister or the couple, hymns are designed to be sung by the whole congregation. Some hymns will work perfectly well with organ accompaniment, but others might need the support of a choir. If worship songs are chosen, it's worth asking whether they would be better accompanied by a worship group, band or keyboard than on the organ.

The Series One service makes no mention of hymns, but *Common Worship* suggests four places where hymns might be sung:

- after the Welcome
- before the Vows
- at the Registration
- after the Prayers

though they may be sung elsewhere (such as, in between two readings). There is also no need to have a full complement of hymns. Two hymns – one after the Welcome and a second following the Prayers – will often be sufficient. It is far better to have two sung well than four sung badly.

Some couples might also suggest including a secular song (either sung live or played from a recording) within the service. Clearly, there should be careful consideration of the lyrics, their appropriateness to an act of Christian worship and of how they fit within the service as a whole.

The pages that follow contain a selection of suitable hymns. Some are time-honoured favourites and others offer newer words, all of which may be sung to well-known tunes. Some of these can be listened to as mp3 files at http://www.yourchurchwedding.org/hymns-media-player.aspx

All my hope on God is founded

Tune: *Michael*

All my hope on God is founded;
He doth still my trust renew.
Me through change and chance he guideth,
Only good and only true.
God unknown,
He alone
Calls my heart to be his own.

Pride of man and earthly glory,
Sword and crown betray his trust;
What with care and toil he buildeth,
Tower and temple, fall to dust.
But God's power,
Hour by hour,
Is my temple and my tower.

God's great goodness aye endureth,
Deep his wisdom passing thought:
Splendour, light and life attend him,
Beauty springeth out of naught.
Evermore,
From his store
New-born worlds rise and adore.

Daily doth the Almighty Giver
Bounteous gifts on us bestow:
His desire our soul delighteth,
Pleasure leads us where we go.
Love doth stand
At his hand;
Joy doth wait on his command.

Still from man to God eternal
Sacrifice of praise be done,
High above all praises praising
For the gift of Christ his Son.
Christ doth call
One and all:
Ye who follow shall not fall.

Robert Bridges 1844–1930

All things bright and beautiful

Tunes: *Royal Oak, All things bright and beautiful*

Refrain:
All things bright and beautiful,
All creatures great and small,
All things wise and wonderful,
The Lord God made them all.

Each little flower that opens,
Each little bird that sings,
He made their glowing colours,
He made their tiny wings:
Refrain

The purple-headed mountain,
The river running by,
The sunset, and the morning
That brightens up the sky:
Refrain

The cold wind in the winter,
The pleasant summer sun,
The ripe fruits in the garden,
He made them every one:
Refrain

The tall trees in the greenwood,
The meadows where we play,
The rushes by the water
We gather every day:
Refrain

He gave us eyes to see them,
And lips that we might tell
How great is God almighty,
Who has made all things well:
Refrain

Cecil Frances Alexander 1818–95

Amazing grace

Tune: *Amazing grace*

Amazing grace! how sweet the sound
That saved a wretch like me!
I once was lost, but now am found,
Was blind, but now I see.

'Twas grace that taught my heart to fear,
And grace my fears relieved;
How precious did that grace appear
The hour I first believed!

Through many dangers, toils and snares,
I have already come;
'Tis grace that brought me safe thus far,
And grace will lead me home.

The Lord has promised good to me,
His word my hope secures;
He will my shield and portion be
As long as life endures.

John Newton 1725–1807

As man and woman we were made*

Tune: *Sussex Carol*

As man and woman we were made
that love be found and life begun:
the likeness of the living God,
unique, yet called to live as one.
Through joy or sadness, calm or strife,
come, praise the love that gives us life.

Joy   Now Jesus lived and gave his love
to make our life and loving new
so celebrate with him today
and drink the joy he offers you
that makes the simple moment shine
and changes water into wine.

Hope   And Jesus died to live again
so praise the love that, come what may,
can bring the dawn and clear the skies,
and waits to wipe all tears away
and let us hope for what shall be
believing where we cannot see.

Peace   Then spread the table, clear the hall
and celebrate till day is done;
let peace go deep between us all
and joy be shared by everyone:
laugh and make merry with your friends
and praise the love that never ends!

Brian Wren 1936–

Alternative words to the same tune

That human life might richer be*

Tune: *Sussex Carol*

That human life might richer be
That children may be named and known,
That love finds its own sanctuary,
That those in love stay not alone.

Refrain:
Praise, praise the Maker, Spirit, Son,
Blessing this marriage now begun.

As two we love are wed this day
And we stand witness to their vow,
We call on God, the Trinity,
To sanctify their pledges now.
Refrain

Parents and families they leave,
Their own new family to make;
And, sharing what their pasts have taught,
They shape it for the future's sake.
Refrain

This is as God meant it to be,
That man and woman should be one
And live in love and love through life,
As Christ on earth has taught and done.
Refrain

Then, bless the bridegroom, bless the bride,
The dreams they dream, the hopes they share;
And thank the Lord whose love inspires
They joy their lips and ours declare.
Refrain

John L. Bell 1949– and Graham Maule 1958–

Be still, for the presence of the Lord*

Tune: *Be still*

Be still for the presence of the Lord,
The Holy One is here;
Come bow before him now
With reverence and fear.
In him no sin is found,
We stand on holy ground;
Be still, for the presence of the Lord,
The Holy One is here.

Be still, for the glory of the Lord
Is shining all around;
He burns with holy fire,
With splendour he is crowned.
How awesome is the sight,
Our radiant King of light!
Be still, for the glory of the Lord
Is shining all around.

Be still, for the power of the Lord
Is moving in this place;
He comes to cleanse and heal,
To minister his grace.
No work too hard for him,
In faith receive from him;
Be still, for the power of the Lord
Is moving in this place.

David J. Evans 1957–

Father, Lord of all creation

Tune: *Abbots Leigh*

Father, Lord of all creation,
ground of Being, Life and Love:

height and depth beyond description
only life in you can prove:
you are mortal life's dependence
thought, speech, sight are ours by grace.
Yours is every hour's existence
sovereign Lord of time and space.

Jesus Christ, the Man for Others
we, your people, make our prayer
help us love as sisters, brothers
all whose burdens we can share.
Where your name binds us together
you, Lord Christ, will surely be;
where no selfishness can sever
there your love may others see.

Holy Spirit, rushing, burning
wind and flame of Pentecost,
fire our hearts afresh with yearning
to regain what we have lost.
May your love unite our action,
nevermore to speak alone:
God, in us abolish faction
God, through us your love make known.

Stewart Cross 1928–1989

For the beauty of the earth

Tunes: *Dix, England's Lane*

For the beauty of the earth,
For the beauty of the skies,
For the love which from our birth
Over and around us lies:

Refrain:
Lord of all, to thee we raise
This our sacrifice of praise.

For the beauty of each hour
Of the day and of the night,
Hill and vale, and tree and flower,
Sun and moon, and stars of light:
Refrain

For the joy of ear and eye,
For the heart and mind's delight,
For the mystic harmony
Linking sense to sound and sight:
Refrain

For the joy of human love,
Brother, sister, parent, child,
Friends on earth, and friends above,
For all gentle thoughts and mild:
Refrain

For each perfect gift of thine
To our race so freely given,
Graces human and divine,
Flowers of earth and buds of heaven:
Refrain

For thy church that evermore
Lifteth holy hands above,
Offering up on every shore
This pure sacrifice of love:
Refrain

F. S. Pierpoint 1835–1917 altered

Great is thy faithfulness*

Tune: *Faithfulness*

Great is thy faithfulness, O God my Father,
There is no shadow of turning with thee;
Thou changest not, thy compassions, they fail not;
As thou hast been, thou for ever wilt be.

Refrain:
Great is thy faithfulness, great is thy faithfulness,
Morning by morning new mercies I see;
All I have needed thy hand hath provided,
Great is thy faithfulness, Lord, unto me.

Summer and winter, and springtime and harvest,
Sun, moon and stars in their courses above,
Join with all nature in manifold witness
To thy great faithfulness, mercy and love.
Refrain

Pardon for sin and a peace that endureth,
Thine own dear presence to cheer and to guide;
Strength for to-day and bright hope for to-morrow,
Blessings all mine, with ten thousand beside!
Refrain

Thomas O. Chisholm 1866–1960

Jerusalem (And did those feet in ancient time)

Tune: *Jerusalem*

And did those feet in ancient time
Walk upon England's mountain green?
And was the holy Lamb of God
On England's pleasant pastures seen?
And did the countenance divine
Shine forth upon our clouded hills?

And was Jerusalem builded here
Among those dark satanic mills?

Bring me my bow of burning gold!
Bring me my arrows of desire!
Bring me my spear! O clouds, unfold!
Bring me my chariot of fire!
I will not cease from mental fight,
Nor shall my sword sleep in my hand,
Till we have built Jerusalem
In England's green and pleasant land.

William Blake 1757–1827

Lord and lover of creation*

Tune: *Westminster Abbey*

Lord and lover of creation,
bless the marriage witnessed now:
sign of lives no longer separate,
sealed by symbol, bound by vow,
celebrating love's commitment
made to live and last and grow.

Praise and gratitude we offer,
for the past which shaped today.
Words which stirred and deepened conscience,
family life, good company,
friends who touched and summoned talent,
nourished all words can't convey.

On your children wed and welcome
here among us, we request
health in home and hearts, and humour
through which heaven and earth are blessed;
open doors and human pleasure,
time for touch and trust and rest.

Take them hence that, in each other,
love fulfilling love shall find
much to share and more to treasure,
such that none dare break or bind
those your name has joined together,
one in body, heart and mind.

John L. Bell 1949– and Graham Maule 1958–

Lord of all hopefulness*

Tune: *Slane*

Lord of all hopefulness, Lord of all joy,
Whose trust, ever childlike, no cares could destroy,
Be there at our waking, and give us, we pray,
Your bliss in our hearts, Lord, at the break of the day.

Lord of all eagerness, Lord of all faith,
Whose strong hands were skilled at the plane and the lathe,
Be there at our labours, and give us, we pray,
Your strength in our hearts, Lord, at the noon of the day.

Lord of all kindliness, Lord of all grace,
Your hands swift to welcome, your arms to embrace,
Be there at our homing, and give us, we pray,
Your love in our hearts, Lord, at the eve of the day.

Lord of all gentleness, Lord of all calm,
Whose voice is contentment, whose presence is balm,
Be there at our sleeping, and give us, we pray,
Your peace in our hearts, Lord, at the end of the day.

Jan Struther 1901–53

Lord of the dance*

Tune: *Lord of the dance*

I danced in the morning
When the world was begun,
And I danced in the moon
And the stars and the sun,
And I came down from heaven
And I danced on the earth,
At Bethlehem
I had my birth.

Dance, then, wherever you may be,
I am the Lord of the Dance, said he,
And I'll lead you all, wherever you may be,
And I'll lead you all in the Dance, said he.

I danced for the Scribe
And the Pharisee,
But they would not dance
And they wouldn't follow me.
I danced for the fishermen,
For James and John –
They came with me
And the Dance went on.
Chorus

I danced on the Sabbath
And I cured the lame;
The holy people
Said it was a shame.
They whipped and they stripped
And they hung me on high,
And they left me there
On a Cross to die.
Chorus

I danced on a Friday
When the sky turned black –
It's hard to dance
With the devil on your back.
They buried my body
And they thought I'd gone,
But I am the Dance,
And I still go on.
Chorus

They cut me down
And I leapt up high;
I am the life
That'll never, never die;
I'll live in you
If you'll live in me –
I am the Lord
Of the Dance, said he.
Chorus

Sydney Carter 1915–2004

Love Divine

Tune: *Blaenwern*

Love Divine, all loves excelling,
Joy of heaven, to earth come down,
Fix in us thy humble dwelling,
All thy faithful mercies crown.
Jesu, thou art all compassion,
Pure unbounded love thou art;
Visit us with thy salvation,
Enter every trembling heart.

Come, almighty to deliver,
Let us all thy grace receive;
Suddenly return, and never,
Never more thy temples leave.

Thee we would be always blessing,
Serve thee as thy hosts above;
Pray, and praise thee, without ceasing,
Glory in thy perfect love.

Finish then thy new creation:
Pure and spotless let us be;
Let us see thy great salvation
Perfectly restored in thee;
Changed from glory into glory
Till in heaven we take our place,
Till we cast our crowns before thee,
Lost in wonder, love, and praise!

Charles Wesley 1707–88

Make me a channel of your peace

Tune: *Channel of Peace (St Francis)*

Make me a channel of your peace.
Where there is hatred let me bring your love;
Where there is injury, your pardon, Lord;
And where there's doubt, true faith in you:

Oh, Master, grant that I may never seek
So much to be consoled as to console;
To be understood as to understand;
To be loved, as to love with all my soul.

Make me a channel of your peace.
Where there's despair in life, let me bring hope;
Where there is darkness, only light;
And where there's sadness, ever joy:

Refrain

Make me a channel of your peace.
It is in pardoning that we are pardoned,
In giving of ourselves that we receive,
And in dying that we're born to eternal life.

Refrain

Sebastian Temple 1928–97 after Francis of Assisi 1182–1226

Morning has broken

Tune: *Bunessan*

Morning has broken,
Like the first morning,
Blackbird has spoken
Like the first bird;
Praise for the singing,
Praise for the morning,
Praise for them springing
Fresh from the Word.

Sweet the rain's new fall,
Sunlit from heaven,
Like the first dewfall
On the first grass;
Praise for the sweetness,
Of the wet garden,
Sprung in completeness
Where his feet pass.

Mine is the sunlight,
Mine is the morning,
Born of the one light
Eden saw play;
Praise with elation,
Praise every morning,
God's re-creation
Of the new day.

Eleanor Farjeon 1881–1965

O praise ye the Lord!

Tune: *Laudate Dominum*

O praise ye the Lord! Praise Him in the height;
Rejoice in his word, ye angels of light;
Ye heavens adore him by whom ye were made,
And worship before him, in brightness arrayed.

O praise ye the Lord! Praise him upon earth,
In tuneful accord, ye sons of new birth;
Praise him who hath brought you his grace from above,
Praise him who hath taught you to sing of his love.

O praise ye the Lord, all things that give sound;
Each jubilant chord re-echo around;
Loud organs, his glory forth tell in deep tone,
And, sweet harp, the story of what he hath done.

O praise ye the Lord! Thanksgiving and song
To him be outpoured all ages along:
For love in creation, for heaven restored,
For grace of salvation, O praise ye the Lord!

H. W. Baker 1821–77 after Psalms 149 and 150

Praise, my soul, the King of heaven

Tune: *Praise my soul*

Praise, my soul, the King of heaven,
To his feet thy tribute bring;
Ransomed, healed, restored, forgiven,
Who like me his praise should sing?
Praise him! Praise him!
Praise him! Praise him!
Praise the everlasting King!

Praise him for his grace and favour
To our fathers in distress;

Praise him still the same for ever,
Slow to chide, and swift to bless.
Praise him! Praise him!
Praise him! Praise him!
Glorious in his faithfulness.

Father-like he tends and spares us;
Well our feeble frame he knows;
In his hands he gently bears us,
Rescues us from all our foes.
Praise him! Praise him!
Praise him! Praise him!
Widely as his mercy flows.

Angels, help us to adore him;
Ye behold him face to face;
Sun and moon, bow down before him,
Dwellers all in time and space:
Praise him! Praise him!
Praise him! Praise him!
Praise with us the God of grace.

H. F. Lyte 1793–1847 after Psalm 103

Praise to the Lord, the almighty

Tune: *Lobe den Herren*

Praise to the Lord, the almighty, the King of creation!
O my soul, praise him, for he is thy health and salvation:
Come ye who hear,
Brothers and sisters, draw near,
Praise him in glad adoration!

Praise to the Lord, who o'er all things so wondrously reigneth,
Shelters thee under his wings, yea, so gently sustaineth:
Hast thou not seen
All that is needful hath been
Granted in what he ordaineth?

Praise to the Lord, who doth prosper thy work and defend thee!
Surely his goodness and mercy shall daily attend thee:
Ponder anew
All the Almighty can do,
He who with love doth befriend thee.

Praise to the Lord! O let all that is in me adore him!
All that hath life and breath come now with praises before him!
Let the amen
Sound from his people again:
Gladly for aye we adore him!

Joachim Neander 1650–80
trans. Catherine Winkworth 1827–78 and others

The grace of life is theirs*

Tune: *Darwall's 148th*

The grace of life is theirs
who on this wedding day
delight to make their vows
and for each other pray.
May they, O Lord, together prove
the lasting joy of Christian love.

Where love is, God abides:
and God shall surely bless
a home where trust and care
give birth to happiness.
May they, O Lord, together prove
the lasting joy of such a love.

How slow to take offence
love is! How quick to heal!
How ready in distress
to know how others feel!
May they, O Lord, together prove
the lasting joy of such a love.

And when time lays its hand
on all we hold most dear,
and life, by life consumed,
fulfils its purpose here:
May we, O Lord, together prove
the lasting joy of Christian love.

Fred Pratt Green 1903–2000

The King of love my Shepherd is

Tune: *Dominus regit me*

The King of love my Shepherd is,
Whose goodness faileth never;
I nothing lack if I am his
And he is mine for ever.

Where streams of living water flow
My ransomed soul he leadeth,
And where the verdant pastures grow
With food celestial feedeth.

Perverse and foolish oft I strayed,
But yet in love he sought me,
And on his shoulder gently laid,
And home, rejoicing, brought me.

In death's dark vale I fear no ill
With thee, dear Lord, beside me;
Thy rod and staff my comfort still,
Thy cross before to guide me.

Thou spread'st a table in my sight;
Thy unction, grace bestoweth;
And O what transport of delight
From thy pure chalice floweth!

And so through all the length of days
Thy goodness faileth never;
Good Shepherd, may I sing thy praise
Within thy house for ever.

H. W. Baker 1821–77 after Psalm 23

Alternative setting of the same text, based on Psalm 23:

The Lord's my shepherd*

Tune: *The Lord's my shepherd*

The Lord's my shepherd, I'll not want.
He makes me lie in pastures green.
He leads me by the still, still waters,
His goodness restores my soul.

And I will trust in you alone.
And I will trust in you alone,
For your endless mercy follows me,
Your goodness will lead me home.

(Descant)
I will trust, I will trust in you.
I will trust, I will trust in you.
Endless mercy follows me,
Goodness will lead me home.

He guides my ways in righteousness,
And He anoints my head with oil,
And my cup, it overflows with joy,
I feast on His pure delights.

And though I walk the darkest path,
I will not fear the evil one,
For You are with me, and Your rod and staff
Are the comfort I need to know.

Stuart Townend 1965– after Psalm 23

We pledge to one another

Tune: *Thaxted*

We pledge to one another,
before the Lord above,
entire and whole and perfect,
this union of our love –
a love that will be patient,
a love that will be wise,
that will not twist with envy,
nor lose itself in lies;
a love that will not falter,
a love to hold us fast,
and bind us to each other
as long as life shall last.

We pray that God will guide us
through all the years to be,
our lives be shaped by courage,
hope and serenity.
Through joy and celebration,
through loneliness and pain,
may loyalty, compassion
and tenderness remain,
that those who share the blessing
of love that cannot cease
may walk the paths of gentleness
into the place of peace.

Jill Jenkins 1937–

Prayers

For the couple

Prayers at your Wedding

An important part of any marriage service is the prayer that is offered for you as you start out on a new chapter of your life together. As well as the priest's prayer for God's blessing on your marriage, prayers are usually said

- thanking God for the love you have for each other
- asking God to help you grow spiritually and understanding God's purpose for your lives
- asking for strength to be faithful to one another
- for the gift of children and your wider family.

The prayers are another part of the service where it might be possible to involve a friend or member of the family, but this should be discussed with the priest at an early stage. As with readings, it's important that anyone asked to take a part in leading prayers is happy and able to do this.

Some of the set forms of prayer from the marriage service are given on pages 70–76. It might also be possible to write your own prayers for the service after discussion with the priest.

For the minister

PRAYERS

All Marriage Services include prayer. In the Series One service, the wording for this is fixed – though many ministers might wish to use additional or alternative prayers. In *Common Worship* a number of forms of prayer (*Pastoral Services* pp 112–13 and 156–168) are given as suggestions, but there is flexibility to use other prayers, possibly written specially for the occasion. In some contexts, it might be appropriate for extempore prayer to be offered during the service.

The prayers provide another very positive opportunity for a minister to work together with the couple during preparation in choosing and / or writing prayers for their wedding. The prayers can be tailored to their own situation or needs and the exercise can be a very fruitful in terms of exploring the Christian faith.

During the service, prayers may be led by a minister other than the officiating priest, or by a member of the congregation. If someone else (e.g. a friend or family member) has offered to write prayers, it's important that they are given clear guidance on length, style and content, and also to make sure that the prayers are seen well in advance of the service!

The prayers end with the Lord's Prayer, said by the whole congregation. In a contemporary language service, this may be said in either its modern or traditional form. If an order of service is being printed, it is always helpful to have the Lord's Prayer printed for the benefit of the congregation.

The prayers that follow are selected from *Common Worship*. They include some longer prayers with a congregational response, and shorter, more specific prayers for the wedding day, the couple and their family.

Some Longer Prayers

A prayer for all people

> Almighty God, look graciously on the world which you have made
> and for which your Son gave his life.
> Bless all whom you make one flesh in marriage.
> May their life together be a sign of your love to this broken world,
> so that unity may overcome estrangement,
> forgiveness heal guilt, and joy overcome despair.
> Lord, in your mercy

All   **hear our prayer.**

> May N and N so live together
> that the strength of their love may reflect your love
> and enrich our common life.
> Lord, in your mercy

All   **hear our prayer.**

> May they be gentle and patient, ready to trust each other,
> and, when they fail, willing to recognize and acknowledge their fault
> and to give and receive forgiveness.
> Lord, in your mercy

All   **hear our prayer.**

> [May N and N be blessed with the gift of children.
> Fill them with wisdom and love as they care for their family.
> Lord, in your mercy

All   **hear our prayer.]**

> May the lonely, the bereaved, and all who suffer want or anxiety,
> be defended by you, O Lord.
> Lord, in your mercy

All   **hear our prayer.**

> May those whose lives are today brought together
> be given wisdom, patience and courage
> to serve one another in Christ's name.
> Lord, in your mercy

All   **hear our prayer.**

May friends and family gathered here,
and those separated by distance,
be strengthened and blessed this day.
Lord, in your mercy
All   **hear our prayer.**

We praise you, merciful God,
for those who have died in the faith of Christ.
May we be strengthened by their example.

Almighty God, you have promised to hear our prayers.
All   **Grant that what we have asked in faith**
we may by your grace receive,
through Jesus Christ our Lord. Amen.

Almighty God, our heavenly Father, we lift up our hearts to you
through Jesus Christ our Lord.
Through him you have made a covenant of grace with your people
by the outpouring of your Holy Spirit.

We praise you for the gift of marriage
in which the love of husband and wife
reveals your purposes of love for the world.

We thank you today for N and N,
for leading them to each other
in friendship and love, commitment and trust,
and for bringing them here for the blessing of their marriage.

Living God,
by the presence of your Holy Spirit,
may they know the risen Christ to be with them now,
as they celebrate this covenant together.
May their lives be a witness to your saving love
in this troubled world.

As you pour out your love,
may they grow together in your sight,
and each be to the other
a companion in joy, a comfort in sorrow and a strength in need.

As you blessed the earthly home at Nazareth
with the presence of your Son,
may their home be a place of security and peace.
[Bless this couple with the gift and care of children,
that they may grow up to know and love you in your Son.]

And bring us all at the last
to that great marriage banquet of your Son
in our home in heaven,
where, with all your saints and angels,
in the glory of your presence,
we will for ever praise you;
through Jesus Christ our Lord.

All   **Amen.**

Thanksgiving

God of love,
we thank you for the gift of marriage and for the joys it brings.
Bless us as we share in this wedding.
We thank you for the love
which has brought N and N to each other
and for their desire to share that
love for the rest of their lives;
through Jesus Christ our Lord.

All   **Amen.**

For discipleship

Eternal God,
without your grace nothing is strong, nothing is sure.
Strengthen N and N with patience, kindness, gentleness
and all other gifts of the Holy Spirit,
so that they may fulfil the vows they have made.

Keep them faithful to each other and to you.
Fill them with such love and joy
that they may build a home of peace and welcome.
Make their life together a sign of Christ's love
   in this broken world,
that unity may overcome estrangement,
forgiveness heal guilt,
and joy conquer despair;
through Jesus Christ our Lord.

All   **Amen.**

For a glimpse of eternal love

Eternal God, our maker and redeemer,
as you once enriched the wedding at Cana
when your Son turned water into wine,
so by his presence now bring your joy to this day.
May we drink deeply from your boundless love
and know in our hearts the delights of your Holy Spirit.
As we honour the union of a man and a woman,
let the love we celebrate today be a sign of your eternal love,
Father, Son, and Holy Spirit.

All   **Amen.**

For marriage as a sign to the world

Almighty God, in whom we live and move and have our being,
look graciously upon the world which you have made
and for which your Son gave his life,
and especially on all whom you make to be one flesh
   in holy marriage.
May their lives together be a sign of your love to this broken world,
so that unity may overcome estrangement,
forgiveness heal guilt,
and joy overcome despair;
through Jesus Christ our Lord.

All   **Amen.**

For the joy of loving

> God our creator,
> we thank you for your gift of sexual love
> by which husband and wife
> may delight in each other
> and share with you the joy of creating new life.
> By your grace may N and N remain lovers,
> rejoicing in your goodness all their days.

All   **Amen.**

For the joy of companionship

> All praise and blessing to you, God of love,
> creator of the universe,
> maker of man and woman in your likeness,
> source of blessing for married life.
> All praise to you, for you have created
>   courtship and marriage,
>   joy and gladness,
>   feasting and laughter,
>   pleasure and delight.
> May your blessing come in full upon N and N.
> May they know your presence
> in their joys and in their sorrows.
> May they reach old age in the company of friends
> and come at last to your eternal kingdom;
> through Jesus Christ our Lord.

All   **Amen.**

For grace and delight

> God of love, ever gracious and kind,
> we pray for N and N as they make the promises of marriage.
> Let them know you
> as the God of mercy and new beginnings,
> who forgives our failures and renews our hope.

May the grace of Christ
be poured into their wedding
for celebration and for joy.
God of love, ever present and faithful,
may N and N know that their marriage is your delight and will.
May the promises they make govern their life together,
as your presence surrounds them,
and your Spirit strengthens and guides them;
through Jesus Christ our Lord.

All   **Amen.**

For faithfulness

God of all grace,
friend and companion,
look in favour on N and N,
and all who are made one in marriage.
In your love deepen their love
and strengthen their wills
to keep the promises they have made,
that they may continue
in life-long faithfulness to each other;
through Jesus Christ our Lord.

All   **Amen.**

For daily following of Christ

Heavenly Father,
we thank you that in our earthly lives
you speak to us of your eternal life:
we pray that through their marriage
N and N may know you more clearly,
love you more dearly
and follow you more nearly,
day by day;
through Jesus Christ our Lord.

All   **Amen.**

For children and family

> Lord of life,
> you shape us in your image,
> and by your gracious gift
> the human family is increased.
> Grant to N and N the blessing of children.
> Fill them with wisdom and love
> as they care for their family,
> so that they and their children
> may know and love you;
> through your Son Jesus Christ our Lord.

All   **Amen.**

For an existing family

> God of all grace and goodness,
> we thank you for this new family,
> and for everything parents and children have to share;
> by your Spirit of peace draw them together
> and help them to be true friends to one another.
> Let your love surround them
> and your care protect them;
> through Jesus Christ our Lord.

All   **Amen.**

For the support of friends

> Holy Spirit of God,
> you know our strength
> and have compassion on our frailty.
> Be with N and N
> in all they undertake.
> And grant that we their friends,
> with all who become their friends,
> may sense and understand their needs;
> through Jesus Christ our Lord.

All   **Amen.**

Alternative vows and prayers

For the couple

At a Church of England wedding, the vows you take must be those printed within one of the authorized Marriage Services. However, there is an option to replace the vows from the *Common Worship* service with one of two alternative forms.

Form 1 (below) adds to the vows a promise by the bride to 'obey' her husband. Deciding to use this form is obviously a matter of personal choice, and views as to how suitable it is in a twenty-first-century context differ from person to person.

The use of Form 2 (below) allows 'traditional language' vows to be used within a modern language service, either with or without a promise to obey.

For the minister

The *Common Worship* Marriage Service includes the option of using one of two alternative forms of marriage vows instead of those printed in the service itself. The first of these (Form 1 below) is in modern language but adds the bride's promise to 'obey'. The second (Form 2) is taken from the *Book of Common Prayer* and is therefore in traditional language. If Form 2 is used, there is a further option to use it without the bride's promise to obey. Ministers are encouraged to spend time discussing the implications of choosing vows in which the bride promises to obey. Most would probably feel that there is little to commend it within a twenty-first-century Christian marriage, but the contrary view is also held by some.

Alternative Vows

Form 1

The bridegroom takes the bride's right hand in his, and says

> I, N, take you, N,
> to be my wife,
> to have and to hold
> from this day forward;
> for better, for worse,
> for richer, for poorer,
> in sickness and in health,
> to love and to cherish,
> till death us do part,
> according to God's holy law.
> In the presence of God I make this vow.

They loose hands.

The bride takes the bridegroom's right hand in hers, and says

> I, N, take you, N,
> to be my husband,
> to have and to hold
> from this day forward;
> for better, for worse,
> for richer, for poorer,
> in sickness and in health,
> to love, cherish, and obey,
> till death us do part,
> according to God's holy law.
> In the presence of God I make this vow.

Form 2

The bridegroom takes the bride's right hand in his, and says

> I, N, take thee, N, to my wedded wife, to have and to hold from this
> day forward, for better for worse, for richer for poorer, in sickness

and in health, to love and to cherish, till death us do part, according to God's holy ordinance; and thereto I plight thee my troth.

They loose hands.

The bride takes the bridegroom's right hand in hers, and says

I, N, take thee, N, to my wedded husband, to have and to hold from this day forward, for better for worse, for richer for poorer, in sickness and in health, to love, cherish, and to obey, till death us do part, according to God's holy ordinance; and thereto I give thee my troth.

[If desired, the word 'obey' may be omitted, as follows

I, N, take thee, N, to my wedded husband, to have and to hold from this day forward, for better for worse, for richer for poorer, in sickness and in health, to love and to cherish, till death us do part, according to God's holy ordinance; and thereto I give thee my troth.]

Prayer at the Giving of the Ring(s)

Heavenly Father, source of everlasting love,
revealed to us in Jesus Christ
    and poured into our hearts through your Holy Spirit;
that love which many waters cannot quench,
    neither the floods drown;
that love which is patient and kind, enduring all things without end;
by your blessing, let these rings be to N and N
symbols to remind them of the covenant made this day
through your grace in the love of your Son
and in the power of your Spirit.

All   **Amen.**

Church of England Marriage Services

The Blessing of the Marriage

One of the following forms may be used

1   God of life and beginnings,
you created man and woman in your likeness
and joined them together in union of body and heart;
God of love and forgiveness,
you loved us in Jesus Christ
who humbled himself to death on a cross;
God of grace and strength,
you bring your people to faith
and fill them with your presence.
Blessed are you, O Lord our God,
for you have created joy and gladness,
pleasure and delight, love, peace and fellowship.
Pour out the abundance of your blessing
upon N and N in their new life together.
Let their love for each other be a seal upon their hearts,
and a crown upon their heads.
Bless them in their work and in their companionship;
awake and asleep,
in joy and in sorrow,
in life and in death.
Finally, in your mercy, bring them to that banquet
where your saints feast for ever in your heavenly home.
We ask this through Jesus Christ your Son, our Lord,
who lives and reigns with you and the Holy Spirit,
one God, now and for ever.

All   **Amen.**

2   All praise and blessing to you, God of love, creator of the
universe,
maker of man and woman in your likeness,
source of blessing for married life.

All praise to you, for you have created
    courtship and marriage,
    joy and gladness,
    feasting and laughter,
    pleasure and delight.
May your blessing come in full upon *N* and *N*.
May they know your presence
in their joys and in their sorrows.
May they reach old age in the company of friends
and come at last to your eternal kingdom,
through Jesus Christ our Lord.

All   **Amen.**

3   Eternal God,
you create us out of love
that we should love you and one another.
Bless this man and this woman, made in your image,
who today become a sign of your faithful love to us
in Christ our Lord.

All   **Amen.**

By your Holy Spirit,
fill bride and bridegroom with wisdom and hope
that they may delight in your gift of marriage
and enrich one another in love and faithfulness;
through Jesus Christ our Lord.

All   **Amen.**

Bring them to that table
where your saints celebrate for ever in your heavenly home;
through Jesus Christ our Lord,
who with you and the Holy Spirit lives and reigns,
one God, for ever and ever.

All   **Amen.**

4   Blessed are you, Lord our God,
         God of love, creator of all.

All   **Blessed be God for ever.**

Bridegroom   Blessed are you, Lord our God,
         you make us in your image and likeness.

All   **Blessed be God for ever.**

Bride   Blessed are you, Lord our God,
         you make man and woman to reflect your glory.

All   **Blessed be God for ever.**

Bridegroom   Blessed are you, Lord our God,
         you make us for joy and promise us life.

All   **Blessed be God for ever.**

Bride   Blessed are you, Lord our God,
         you create a people to know your love.

All   **Blessed be God for ever.**

Minister   May *N* and *N* enjoy the blessing of your kingdom.
         Give them faith and joy in their marriage.
         Blessed are you, Lord our God,
         you give joy to bride and groom.

All   **Blessed be God for ever.**

         May their love be fruitful
         and their home a place of peace.
         Blessed are you, Lord our God,
         you make marriage a sign of your love.

All   **Blessed be God for ever.**

         May they know the love of the Father,
         the life of the Son,
         and the joy of the Spirit.
         Blessed are you, Lord our God,
         Lover, Beloved and Friend of Love.

All   **Blessed be God for ever.**

5   *This form may be added to any of the preceding blessings, or may be used
    on its own*

Blessed are you, heavenly Father.
All **You give joy to bridegroom and bride.**

Blessed are you, Lord Jesus Christ.
All **You bring life to the world.**

Blessed are you, Holy Spirit of God.
All **You bind us together in love.**

Blessed are you, Father, Son, and Holy Spirit, now and for ever.
All **Amen.**

Acknowledgements

Text

Hymns

'Be still, for the [presence of the Lord]', David Evans © 1986, Thankyou Music

Please email: tym@kingsway.co.uk or call 01323 437712 for further information.

'Father, Lord of all creation', Stewart Cross 1989 © Mrs Mary Cross, Honeybee House, Brigsteer, Kendal, Cumbria LA8 8AP. Reproduced by permission.

'Great is thy faithfulness', Thomas O. Chisholm © 1923 renewed 1951, Hope Publishing Company. Administered by CopyCare.

'Lord and lover of creation', John L. Bell and Graham Maule, in *Love from Below*, Wild Goose Publications © 1989, WGRG, Iona Community.

'Lord of all hopefulness', Jan Struther, in *Enlarged Songs of Praise* © 1931, Oxford University Press, reproduced by permission. All rights reserved.

'Lord of the dance', Sidney Carter © 1963 Stainer & Bell Ltd.

'Morning has broken', Eleanor Farjeon © David Higham Associates.

'Make me a channel of your peace', Sebastian Temple © 1967 OCP Publications c/o Calamus:www.decanimusic.co.uk. All rights reserved.

'That human life might richer be', in *Love from Below* © 1989, WGRG, Iona Community.

'The grace of life is theirs', Fred Pratt Green © Copyright 1970 Stainer & Bell Ltd.

'The Lord's my shepherd', Stuart Townend © 1996 Thankyou Music. As the words to this song are in copyright they may only be reproduced in your Order of Service by permission of the copyright holder, Thankyou Music. Please email: tym@kingsway.co.uk or call 01323 437712 for further information.

'We pledge to one another', Jill Jenkins © Jill Jenkins, 61 Lakeside Road, London N13 4PS.